WATER

Angela Royston

Heinemann Library
Chicago, Illinois

Customer Service 888-454-2279

Visit our website at www.heinemannlibrary.com

Designed by bigtop
Originated by Ambassador Litho
Printed and bound in Hong Kong/China

06 05 04 03 02
10 9 8 7 6 5 4 3 2 1

Library of Congress Cataloging-in-Publication Data

Royston, Angela.
    Water / Angela Royston.
        p. cm. -- (My world of science)
Includes bibliographical references and index.
    ISBN 1-58810-247-5
    1. Water--Juvenile literature. [1. Water.] I. Title.
    GB662.3 .R69 2001
    553.7--dc21
                                        00-012877
Acknowledgments
The author and publishers are grateful to the following for permission to reproduce copyright material:
Toby Adamson/Still Pictures: p. 25; John Callan, p. 11; Trevor Clifford, pp. 4, 9, 10, 12, 13, 16, 19, 21, 22, 23, 26; Corbis, pp. 5, 6, 7, 14, 15, 17, 24, 27; Eye Ubiquitous, p. 18; Robert Harding, p. 29; Robert Royston, p. 8; Stone, pp. 20, 28.

Cover photograph reproduced with permission of Ray Massey/Stone.

Every effort has been made to contact copyright holders of any material reproduced in this book. Any omissions will be rectified in subsequent printings if notice is given to the publisher.

Some words are shown in bold, like this. You can find out what they mean by looking in the glossary.

Contents

What Is Water?

Water is usually a **liquid.** A liquid does not have a shape of its own. It always takes the shape of its **container.**

Water is a clear liquid. Water can also be a **solid,** called ice. It can also be a **gas,** called steam. Ice is very cold, and steam is very hot.

Where Water Comes From

When it rains, water **flows** off the land into streams and rivers. Streams and rivers flow across the land into lakes and oceans.

water evaporates

rain

Some of the water in lakes, oceans, and rivers **evaporates.** This means it changes into **gas.** This gas floats into the air and forms new rain clouds.

Water for Life

People, plants, and animals all need water to stay alive. Some farmers spray their plants with water to make them grow better.

All food has water in it. Fruit and vegetables have lots of water in them. Squeeze an orange to see how much juice you can get. Most of it is water.

Using Water

We use water at home for washing clothes, dishes, ourselves, and other things. Soap makes washing easier.

Firefighters use water to put out fires.
They pump the water on the flames
through long hoses.

Flowing Water

Water always tries to **flow** downhill. The **steeper** the slope, the faster water flows. What will happen if this girl tips the bottle more?

You cannot make water flow uphill on its own. When you drink through a straw, you have to suck the water up into your mouth.

Ice

Water can be found as a **liquid,** a **gas,** and a **solid.** Ice is frozen water. It is a solid, so it keeps its shape. This statue has been cut from a block of ice.

Thermometers measure **temperature** in degrees. Water freezes into ice at 32 degrees **Fahrenheit.** The ice will melt when the temperature rises above 32 degrees.

Heating Water

When water is heated, it slowly turns into **gas.** When it reaches 212 degrees **Fahrenheit,** it begins to boil. Be careful—boiling water **scalds.**

When water boils, bubbles of gas form in the water. The bubbles rise to the top of the water and burst. The gas drifts up into the air.

Steam

You cannot see the **gas** in the air, but you can see steam. Steam is made when water gas turns back into tiny water **droplets.**

Water droplets form at other times too. If you breathe on a mirror, it will become misty. The mist is made of tiny water droplets.

Drying

Wet hair can be dried with a hair dryer. The water in your hair slowly changes into **gas.** The gas drifts into the air and your hair dries.

These children are measuring the size of a puddle as it **evaporates.** They measure it every 20 minutes. It gets smaller and smaller as it dries.

Floating and Sinking

Some things float when you put them in water. Most light things float. Most heavy things sink. You can test different things to see which ones will float.

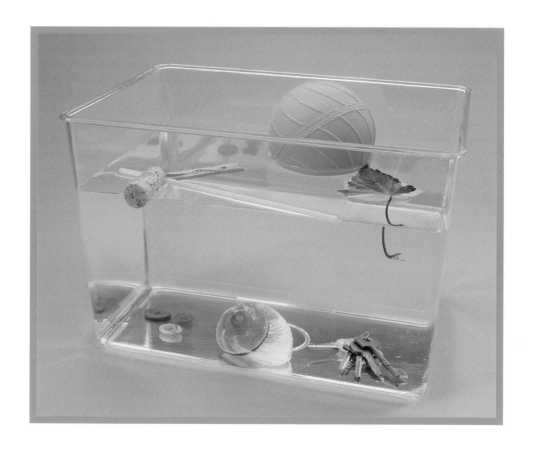

The button is light. The clothespin is heavier than the button. The button sinks. The clothespin floats. Why?

Light for Its Size

Something floats if it is light for its size.
This ship is big and heavy but it floats.
That is because it is filled with air, and
air is very light.

These heavy logs are floating on the
river. Wood floats because there is lots
of air trapped inside it.

Water Pushes Back

When you put something into water, it pushes some of the water away. The water then pushes back. It is hard to push the balloon under the water.

When you lie on water, the water pushes up and makes you float. This is just like when the water pushed back against the balloon.

Moving Through Water

To move through water, you must pull the water backward to push yourself forward. When you swim, your hands and arms pull the water back.

Boats also move forward by pulling the water backward. These people pull the paddles back to push the canoes forward.

Glossary

container something that you can put things in, for example, a box or a jar

droplet very small drop

evaporate when a liquid changes into a gas

Fahrenheit scale for measuring temperature

flow to move smoothly

gas something that is invisible and does not have a shape. Steam is a gas.

liquid something that is wet and takes the shape of its container. Water is a liquid.

scald to burn with hot water or steam

solid something that has a size and shape. An ice cube is a solid.

steep when a slope rises or falls very sharply

temperature how hot or cold something is

thermometer something that tells how hot or cold something is

More Books to Read

Asch, Frank. *Water.* San Diego, Calif.: Harcourt Brace Trade Publishers, 2000.

Hewitt, Sally. *Water.* Danbury, Conn.: Children's Press, 2000.

MacDonald, Fiona. *Water.* Danbury, Conn.: Franklin Watts, 2000. An older reader can help you with this book.

Index